VEHICLES ON THE JOB

FARM QUADS

ON THE FARM

by Samantha Bell

Cherry Lake Press

Published in the United States of America
by Cherry Lake Publishing
Ann Arbor, Michigan
www.cherrylakepublishing.com

Reading Adviser: Beth Walker Gambro, MS, Ed., Reading Consultant, Yorkville, IL
Content Adviser: Louis Teel, Professor of Heavy Equipment Operating, Central Arizona College

Photo Credits: © michael garner/Shutterstock, Anatolir/Shutterstock, cover, title page; © Deb Drury/iStock.com, 4; © Pierrette Guertin/Shutterstock, 6; © ChameleonsEye/Shutterstock, 8; © logoboom/Shutterstock, 10; © Jim Lambert/Shutterstock, 12; © mtneer_man/Flickr, 14; © Frances Valdes/iStock.com, 16; © David P. Lewis/Shutterstock, 18; © Odua Images/Shutterstock, 20

Cherry Lake Press is an imprint of Cherry Lake Publishing Group.

Library of Congress Cataloging-in-Publication Data has been filed and is available at catalog.loc.gov

Cherry Lake Press would like to acknowledge the work of the Partnership for 21st Century Learning, a Network of Battelle for Kids. Please visit Battelle for Kids online for more information.

Printed in the United States of America

Note from Publisher: Websites change regularly, and their future contents are outside of our control. Supervise children when conducting any recommended online searches for extended learning opportunities.

TABLE OF CONTENTS

NO PLACE OFF-LIMITS

ATVs are all-**terrain** vehicles. They are also called quads. Many farmers use them.

Quads can go all over the farm. They can go across fields. They can go through woods.

LOOK

Look at the picture of a farm quad. What features look like they help it drive anywhere on the farm?

SUZUKI
SUZUKI
KINGQUAD
TEX

BUILT FOR WORK

One or 2 people can ride a quad. Quads help farmers do their work.

Farmers use quads to get their work done faster, and to travel where they can't drive a truck. They can check on their **crops**.

They use them to herd **livestock**.

CONNECT

How else have you seen farmers herding livestock?

SporTrak Pro
MAGELLAN
OUT IN
LIGHTS GPS

QUAD ADD-ONS

Farmers can add tools to quads. This one has a **GPS**. Other quads pull tools to dig through the dirt.

Quads can pull wagons.
Farmers can move heavy things.

THINK

Why do you think GPS would be helpful on a farm quad?

POLICE
POLICE
ONT
06VV6

OTHER USES

Quads are not only used on farms. Police officers and other people use them, too.

The work is finished.
Time to ride for fun!

FIND OUT MORE

Go online with an adult to find videos of farm quads. Write down some things you **see** and **hear**.

Then, write what you **think** about those things. **Make a connection** to something else you know.

Next, write what you **wonder** about farm quads from the videos. What would you like to learn more about?

GLOSSARY

crops (KRAHPS) plants that are grown as food or for other uses

GPS (GEE PEE ESS) a digital map system

livestock (LIVE-stahk) farm animals

terrain (tuh-RAYN) the surface of an area of land

INDEX

ABOUT THE AUTHOR

Samantha Bell has written over 100 books for children. She lives in South Carolina with her family and pets.